AD 800	VIKINGS	EUROPE

AD 800

VIKINGS

789 First Viking attacks on England

834 Vikings raid the great market town of Dorestad in the Netherlands

850 Swedes begin to settle in East Baltic and Russia

860 Discovery of Iceland

874 First settlers in Iceland

886 King Alfred defeats Guthrum; Danes allowed to settle in the Danelaw

900

911 Scandinavians settle in Normandy

982 Eirik the Red discovers Greenland

1000

995–1000 Olaf Tryggvason, King of Norway

1003 Leif Eiriksson lands in North America

1030 King Olaf of Norway killed at Battle of Stiklastad

1047 Harald Hardrada becomes King of Norway

1066 Harald Hardrada killed at Battle of Stamford Bridge in England, by King Harold of England. Duke William of Normandy kills Harold of England at the Battle of Hastings and becomes King William I of England

1066

EUROPE

800 Charlemagne, King of the Franks, is crowned Holy Roman Emperor in western Europe

843 Treaty of Verdun divides the Frankish empire between Charlemagne's grandsons

871 Alfred the Great becomes King of Wessex

906 Magyars from the East invade Germany

911 Charles the Simple gives the Viking leader Rollo land in Normandy

955 Otto I of Germany ends the westward advance of the Magyars at the Battle of Lech

987 Hugh Capet elected King of France; foundation of the Capetian Dynasty

1002 Ethelred II of England orders the slaughter of all Danish settlers in southern England

1042 Edward the Confessor becomes King of England

1066 Edward the Confessor dies, Harold II crowned King of England

ISLAM

803 Harun al-Raschid, Caliph of Baghdad destroys the Barmakids, the Persian Dynasty that administers his empire

827 Arabs begin conquest of the islands of Sicily and Sardinia

838 Arabs attack Marseilles and establish a base in southern Italy

843 Arabs capture Messina

859 Arabs complete conquest of Sicily

869 Arabs capture Malta

888 Arabs establish a camp in Provence in France

922 Fatimid Dynasty seizes Morocco

970 The Seljuk Turks become Muslim and occupy most of Persia

980 Arabs begin settling along the eastern coast of Africa

983 The Caliph of Egypt rules over Palestine and southern Syria

1054 Abdallah ben Yassim begins the Muslim conquest of West Africa

1055 The Seljuks seize Baghdad

1061 Muslim Almoravid Dynasty in North Africa; later conquers Spain

ELSEWHERE

821 Conquest of Tibet by the Chinese

832 Nanchao, a state in south China destroys the kingdom of the Pyu people, the earliest known inhabitants of Burma

850 Acropolis of Zimbabwe built in eastern Africa

900 Mayas emigrate to the Yucatan Peninsula of Mexico

907–960 End of T'ang Dynasty in China; civil war follows

920–1050 Golden Age of Ghana empire

939 Civil wars break out in Japan

960 Sung Dynasty in China

987 New Mayan empire established in Yucatan with its capital at Mayapan

995–1028 Golden age of the arts in Japan

1000s Gunpowder perfected by the Chinese

1043 Mandingo empire of Jenne founded in West Africa

AD 800

900

1000

1066

The Vikings

WARWICK PRESS

Contents

Top: Detail of a carved head from the frame of the Oseberg wagon. Centre: The Vikings were expert wood carvers. This strange beast was probably intended to frighten away evil spirits. Below: A runic stone in Sweden. Previous page: A rock crystal pendant.

Editorial

Author
Robin Place

Editor
Jacqui Bailey

Illustrators
Richard Hook
Jeff Burn
Oliver Frey
Carlo Tora

Published 1980 by Warwick Press,
730 Fifth Avenue, New York, New York, 10019.

First published in Great Britain by Longman Group Limited in 1980.

Copyright © 1980 by Grisewood & Dempsey Ltd.

Printed in Hong Kong
by South China Printing Co.
6 5 4 3 2 1   All rights reserved

Library of Congress Catalog Card No.80-50038

ISBN 0-531-09170-8

The Vikings

Above: A silver amulet in the shape of a hammer, decorated with a face with large staring eyes. The face and the hammer shape both represent the god Thor.
Below: The Viking fortress at Trelleborg in Denmark. In the center of the picture is a reconstruction of one of the boat-shaped houses in which the warriors lived.

The Viking Age lasted for about 300 years, from AD 800 to 1100. It was a time when fleets of swift ships with square sails and carved dragon prows brought fierce raiders to rob and plunder throughout western Europe. However, the Vikings were not only robbers and pirates. With their remarkable ships and skills of navigation they explored many new lands. Their love of travel and adventure led them far to the east, to Russia and the great city of Constantinople. In the west, they braved the dangers of the Atlantic to set up colonies in Iceland and Greenland, and they were the first Europeans to discover America.

In spite of their reputation, the Vikings had a great respect for law. They had one of the first forms of parliament. Women had many more rights than in most other societies of the time and even slaves could earn their freedom. Perhaps most surprising of all was the fact that the Vikings were great poets and storytellers. Their world was rich with color and ornament, and there were many legends of heroic deeds and great adventures.

People of the North

The Vikings came from cold lands which stretch far into the north. Large areas are covered with snow and ice, and mountains and forests. Life was often difficult for the people who lived in these lands, but the Vikings were strong and they were good fighters.

Above: The head of a Viking warrior. It is carved from a piece of elkhorn and forms the handle of a stick.

Below: The Vikings in Norway had very little land for farming. Most of it lay in small strips along the coastline of the fjords.

The Scandinavian lands of Norway, Sweden and Denmark lie in the north of Europe, reaching from beyond the Arctic Circle as far south as the latitude of northern England. In mid-summer, in the far north, the Sun does not sink below the horizon at all. In mid-winter there are only a few hours of daylight each day. In the south, where most people live, the climate is not very different from that of the northern United States.

About the year 800, there seems to have come a time when there were simply too many people in Scandinavia. There was not enough land to produce food for them all, especially in Norway and Sweden. In the north of Norway, mountains rise to 2560 meters (8400 feet). Since nearly twenty-five per cent of the country was covered with pine forests, only three per cent of the whole country could be cultivated. This was along the strips of land that lay around the coasts, mainly in the south. In summer, cattle could be driven up to the mountain pastures, but they had to be brought back down to the lowlands in the winter. Most of the people had to be fishermen as well as farmers.

Sweden is a great plain, with mountains only in the north along the border with Norway. In the Viking Age over half the land was covered with dense forests. Only nine per cent of the land could be farmed, again in the south. Denmark is also a low-lying country, but there was better land for farming. Half the country had rich soil on which crops could be grown. The other half was poorer soil but it grew grass that was good for pasture.

Land at home was therefore in short supply, and many Scandinavians moved away with their families and household goods to set up colonies in Iceland, Greenland and in Russia. Others went raiding in the neighboring lands of the British Isles and France. They would often use the wealth they looted to buy land in these countries, and many people who came first as raiders stayed as farmers.

The Vikings abroad

In the Viking Age the people of Norway, Sweden and Denmark did not think of themselves as belonging to a particular country. All Scandinavians spoke the same language, very like the language spoken in Iceland today, and they moved freely from one district to another. If a chief or king in one part of Scandinavia was known to be generous in rewarding his warriors with gold and silver, men from all three countries might become his followers. A Scandinavian who went raiding was called a "Viking". Today

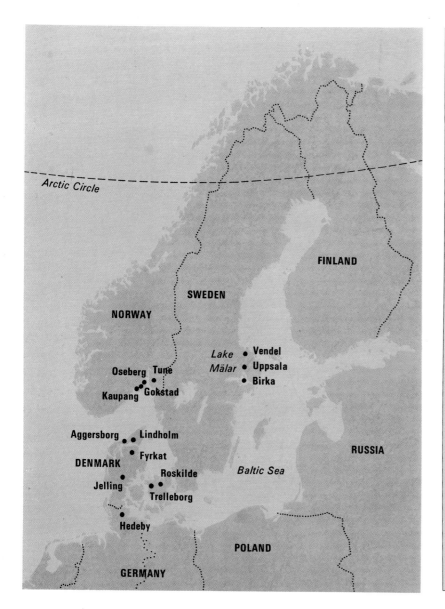

we use this word to describe all the people who lived in Scandinavia between 800 and 1100, but originally Vikings were men who left their homes and went abroad. We do not know the exact meaning of the word *viking*. There are a number of words from which the name could have come. It might have meant "the man from the bay", as *vik* was a word for "bay" or "creek". There was also *vikja*, a word which meant to go fast, or to travel away from home.

The Anglo-Saxons, who fought the Vikings for many years, simply called them "Northmen". The Franks in France also called them Northmen, or "Normans". The Germans called them *arcomanni*, "ship-men", and the Arabs of Spain knew them as *el-Majus*, "the heathen". Only the Irish monks saw a difference between their enemies. They called the Norwegians the "White Foreigners", the *Finn-gaill*, and the Danes the "Black Foreigners", the *Dubh-gaill*. Whatever name they were known by one thing is clear, in an astonishingly short period of time this little-known race of people from the north became a major influence throughout western Europe.

A piece of horn filled with silver coins and ornaments. Precious possessions were buried with the dead for use in the next life.

9

The Viking World

A Viking might be a king, a farmer or a slave, but everyone had to obey a strict code of laws.

The Vikings carved scenes from their daily lives and their legends onto large stones. This picture-stone comes from Gotland in Sweden. It shows the god Odin on his eight-legged horse.

The most important people in the Viking world were the kings and their families. To be a king a man had to be of royal blood. The ancestors of a king were known and listed in his *saga*, the story of his life and deeds. Many Viking kings claimed to be descended from gods. There was an old belief that the powers of the king helped the land to give good harvests, the sea to give a lot of fish, and the people to win battles. If there was famine or battles were lost the king became unpopular and could be driven out. At the start of the Viking Age there were many families in different parts of Scandinavia who ruled as kings. Gradually, one family in each of the Scandinavian lands of Norway, Sweden and Denmark fought its way to power.

Next in line to the kings were the *jarls*. A jarl was an important landowner and warrior. He was not of royal blood, but could rule a large area of land. A jarl might even rule for a time in the place of an unpopular king, but he would never call himself a king. A jarl looked after his people, and gave them advice when they came to him with their problems.

The largest group of Vikings were *karls*, free-born men. A karl could be a rich chief or a poor farmer. The fighting men in raiding parties were karls who wanted adventure and loot. Others became merchants and went away to see the world and make their fortune. Karls who were craftsmen would work at a king's court or in the house of a jarl.

Every household had many slaves, or *thralls*. Some held important positions, such as steward or housekeeper. If thralls had children they were automatically thralls too. People who were captured on raids were sold as thralls, but this could also happen to karls who could not pay their debts. Thralls could be given their freedom if they served their masters and mistresses well, or were brave in battle. Then they were given land to farm and could buy and sell, and arrange their own marriages. Many thralls were also allowed to earn silver to buy their freedom.

The laws of the land

The Vikings had a great respect for law, and the worst punishment of all was to be made an outlaw. Many laws were about compensation, payment of silver when a person or his thrall was killed or injured. A murderer could be caught and killed by the family of the dead man. However, in many cases the family of the murderer and of his victim went to a court and the compensation in silver was worked out.

Below: Part of a reconstruction of a tapestry found on the Oseberg ship. The figures shown here, with their wagons and horses, may be taking part in some kind of burial ceremony.

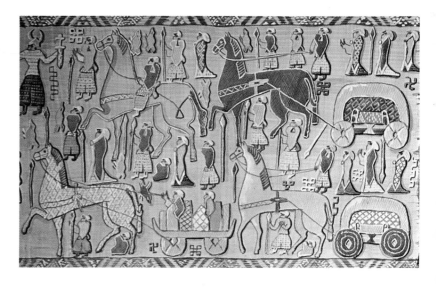

The amount would depend on the reasons for the murder. A man could also be outlawed for killing, or sent abroad in exile for three years.

Most lawsuits were heard at the *Thing*, a meeting of free men that was held out of doors. Things could be summoned whenever necessary. There were local meetings and larger, district Things. Everyone met in a large open space, usually near a temple. There were many disputes about property and about the division of property after a divorce. Things were an important part of social life. People who lived far apart had a chance to meet. Marriages were arranged, sagas were told and traders sold all kinds of goods. It was a fair and a market place as well as an assembly.

Marriage and divorce

When a young man was able to support a wife, his family would arrange a marriage for him. His father would suggest the daughter of a man of equal rank and wealth. The young man would not speak to the girl, but his father, or a friend, would make the proposal to the girl's parents. This might be the first time that the young man and the girl had met. Some parents asked their daughter whether or not she wanted to marry the young man, but many girls were not given any choice.

On festival days and in the evenings when work was finished, the Vikings liked to play board games and games with dice. These gaming counters are made of glass and were found in Viking graves at Birka in Sweden.

Sometimes a marriage ended in divorce. A wife had equal rights in sharing the property and could get a divorce if she was ill-treated. Getting a divorce was fairly simple. The husband or wife had to say that they wanted a divorce in front of witnesses in their house and at the Thing. Then a woman could take her property and return to her family. Both the man and woman were then free to marry again.

Women played a very important part in Viking society. A married woman could do business on her husband's behalf, shaking hands to seal a bargain like a man. She could influence her husband in his affairs. Some wives stopped their husbands from fighting and persuaded them to go to law to settle a dispute. Other wives drove their husbands to take revenge when they were wronged.

DUELING AND ORDEALS

Some lawsuits were settled by dueling. A cloak 3.5 meters (over 11 feet) long was pegged to the ground and the corners were marked with hazel rods. Each man had a friend to hold a shield in front of him while he fought with a sword. The man who had been challenged struck first. If blood fell on the cloak the fight could be stopped and the wounded man lost the case. If a man stepped outside the hazel rods he was treated as if he had run away. He would be called *nithing*, a "coward".

Dueling was not a fair way to decide a lawsuit. A strong young man could challenge an old man. If the old man would not agree to fight he lost his case, even if he was right.

People could also prove their innocence by agreeing to an ordeal. Sometimes this meant placing a hand in boiling water or walking on red-hot iron plowshares. If the wound healed quickly the person was believed to be innocent.

Life on the Farm

Most people were farmers in the Vikings Age. Even raiders and merchants used their wealth to buy land to farm.

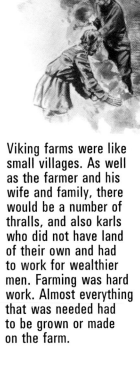

Many men might go trading or raiding abroad in the summer, but if they were farmers, they would always return from their journeys in time to bring in the harvest. When a man was away, his wife would be in charge of the farm. She guarded the keys to the storehouses and was responsible for feeding and clothing the people in the household. Nearly everything they needed was made or grown on the farm. It was terrible for a man to have a lazy wife or for a woman to marry a man who was a bad farmer.

A Viking farm had a number of buildings often in two groups, the living quarters and the farm buildings. In places where there were plenty of trees the buildings were made of wood. Where there were few trees, as in the Orkney and Shetland islands, walls were built of turves laid on top of earth or stones.

The largest building was the long *stofa*, or hall. The roof was supported on two rows of posts down the middle. An important part of the hall was the fireplace, which was usually in the center between the two rows of posts. Everyone ate in the hall in the evening, and guests could spend the night there beside the warm fire. It was the dining room, sitting room and spare bedroom. Tables were carried in for each meal and placed in front of benches built along the long walls. In the center of each row of benches was a high seat, with carved posts, or pillars, reaching up to the roof. The owner of the house sat in the high seat on the north side. His chief guest sat in the high seat opposite. The most important people in the household sat nearest the high-seats. Women sat on the cross-bench along one of the short walls. They also served the food and the drink.

Food was cooked in the *skali* or *eld-hus* (fire house). Women cooked the joints of meat, ground grain into flour and baked bread, made porridge and gruel, cooked cabbages, turnips, peas and beans and brewed ale. Food and tools were kept in small storehouses called *burs*, which had lofts where people slept.

The farm buildings would include *byres*, sheds for sheep and cattle. Byres had a stone floor and a drain so that they could be washed down. There were barns where hay was stored and plows and tools were kept, granaries for grain and a smithy. Many farmers were skilled blacksmiths.

Daily life

Except for the wealthiest landowners, the whole family worked on the farm as well as their thralls. There was always plenty to do. The fields had to be plowed and planted with rye, oats, wheat and barley. There were cattle and sheep and sometimes pigs and goats to be cared for. Women milked the cows and made butter, cheese and a delicious type of creamy curds called *skyr*.

In summer the cattle were driven up to graze on the rich mountain pastures. Sometimes the household would move to a small farm up in the mountains called a *shieling*. Here, they would tend the sheep and cattle during the summer months. Sheepdogs helped shepherds to herd the flocks, and wool from the sheep was brought back for the women to make into clothes. In the fall, corn

Viking farms were like small villages. As well as the farmer and his wife and family, there would be a number of thralls, and also karls who did not have land of their own and had to work for wealthier men. Farming was hard work. Almost everything that was needed had to be grown or made on the farm.

was reaped, threshed with flails and winnowed. It was carried into the granaries to be stored for the winter.

There were many other routine tasks to be done. Skilled thralls were sent off into the woods as charcoal burners. Charcoal was needed for the furnace in the smithy. Other thralls collected driftwood for building and for firewood. Peat was cut for fuel where wood was in short supply. Animals were hunted for food and their skins were used to make warm cloaks.

Along the coast men hunted seals. The meat was eaten and the skin cut up into strips for ropes. Fishing was another very important source of food. Much of this fish, as well as some meat, was dried, smoked or salted in the summer, and carefully stored so that it could be eaten in winter.

In the evening, when the work was finished, there was time to play games. The Vikings played a form of chess, and other games using a dice. Sometimes the hall would be hushed while everyone listened to a storyteller, or a visitor told the latest news. There were often visitors at a farm. Traveling craftsmen and traders stayed for a time. Men selling salt made from seawater would be especially welcome.

13

Towns and Trading

Trading was an important part of life. As well as their goods, traders often brought news from other countries. Trading centers became rich towns and people came to them from far and wide.

All traders were welcomed at the courts of kings and chiefs wherever they went. This was partly because of the goods they brought, but perhaps more important was the news they collected while they were on their journeys. News of the outside world was hard to get in the days before printed newspapers. Traders were highly respected. They could become very rich if they did not lose their goods through shipwreck or robbery. Some people spent their whole lives as traders. They did not sell their goods in a shop, but traveled around the Scandinavian world carrying their goods to different towns and markets.

Other traders were only part-time merchants. They owned land of their own and spent the winter on their farms. In the spring they left their homes in the care of their wives and families and set off in their ships. They returned home at harvest time after selling their goods.

Market towns

The first towns in Scandinavia grew up as markets where traders could sell their goods peacefully. Norwegian merchants went mainly to England and Ireland. They brought weapons and ornaments from there back to Kaupang. Kaupang was on the coast of Norway, on the west shore of Oslofjord. Goods for export were made at Kaupang by metalworkers and weavers. Smooth soapstone dishes were also carved there.

From Kaupang, a trader could sail to Hedeby. Hedeby was the great trade center for the whole of Scandinavia. It was inland, at the south of the Jutland peninsula in Denmark, and was safe

Above: The first Viking coins were made at the beginning of the 9th century. This one and the one on the opposite page both come from Birka in Sweden.

Above: These pottery vessels were found in merchants' graves at Birka. They were not made in Scandinavia, but were brought in as foreign goods for trading.

Right: The site at Birka. The remains of the rampart that protected the town on the landward side can still be seen today.

from sea raiders. Ships from the Baltic could reach its harbor by rowing up river. Ships from the North Sea could come up the River Eider to within 17 kilometers (10 miles). Goods were then unloaded and trundled to Hedeby in carts. The way was protected against attacks from the south by a massive rampart, called the "Danewirke".

All sorts of things could be bought at Hedeby. Millstones for grinding corn were needed in every house. Here the very best were found. They were made from the special hard rock of the Rhineland. From England, France and Germany came fine pots, delicate glassware and swords. From Poland there were Slav prisoners for sale as slaves, and from the north there were all kinds of rich furs and useful soapstone vessels.

Hedeby was the largest Scandinavian town. The eastern side was open to a lake. On land, it was protected by a rampart over 9 meters (30 feet) high, with a deep moat outside. There were three tunnel-like entrances through the rampart, which were edged with planks and paved with stone. Inside the rampart were many wooden houses, warehouses and workshops. Blacksmiths and bronzesmiths, glassworkers and weavers worked there. Some houses were built of wooden planks. Others had a timber frame and walls made of wattle and daub (hurdles of twigs and sticks plastered with clay). Roofs were made of reed thatch.

The town of Birka

The third great Viking town was Birka, in Sweden. Birka was on the northwest part of a large island in Lake Mälar. From Birka, rivers and lakes led into central and northern Sweden, so that goods could be taken north, south, east and west. This is why Birka became an important town.

Beside the lake there were oak jetties where ships could tie up and unload. Nearby, on level ground, was the town, with houses made from wooden planks or wattle and daub, as at Hedeby. The town was protected by a fort on a great rock over 30 meters (100 feet) high, from which guards had a good view far down the lake. On the landward side of the town was a rampart with six wooden towers.

Outside the town was a great cemetery of more than 2000 graves. By studying the objects that have been found buried with the dead, we know that most of Birka's trade was with the Swedish colonies on the River Volga in Russia. Thousands of silver Arabian coins were found, most of them brought from Russia. There were traces of silk patterned with gold from China, and an amethyst ring from south of the Caspian Sea. There was some trade with the west, but the routes to England were closed in about AD 850 because of raids on the ships by pirates. Before this, fine wool cloth came from Frisia (now the Netherlands), and pots and glassware from the Rhineland. Merchants may have obtained furs and articles carved from reindeer antlers and walrus ivory in exchange for foreign goods. However, it is more likely that they spent their Arabian silver on the imported goods they found at Birka, such as weapons, luxury foods and valuable ornaments to wear.

BUYING AND SELLING

The Vikings paid for anything they wanted to buy with silver and gold. The price of timber, slaves or costly clothing was weighed out in *marks* and *aurar*. One mark was eight aurar. Gold was worth eight times as much as silver. One mark of silver could buy four cows. A good sword could cost four marks of silver or half a mark of gold.

Every merchant carried a pair of bronze scales. They were made to fold away in a little round box. The merchant would put his weights in one pan of his scales and his customer would put his silver bars into the other. He might add some Arabian coins to make up the weight.

Clothes and Ornaments

Both men and women liked to wear richly colored clothes and a lot of bright jewelry.

The Vikings cared a great deal about their personal appearance. Clothes were often described in the sagas, and it was important for a chief or king to be richly dressed. He was also expected to reward his followers with presents of ornaments or suits of clothes. People loved to wear bright colours. Blue, red, green and purple garments looked lovely with the silver and gold jewelry worn by both men and women.

Clothes were made of many materials. Coarse white cloth called *vathmal* was woven at home from sheep's wool. It was used for traveling cloaks, blankets and tunics worn by thralls. Frisian wool cloth was finer. It was imported from Frisia (now the Netherlands). Linen, made from flax, was both imported and woven at home. Clothing for special occasions was made of *skarlat*, an imported red cloth. There was also *pell*, a kind of velvet, and *silki*, silk

Fashions seem to have changed very little during the Viking Age. The sagas often describe the clothes people wore and from them we can form quite a clear picture of what the Vikings looked like. The couple shown here would be typical of a landowner or trader and his wife.

Left: This silver arm ring comes from Gotland in Sweden. Arm rings were made of solid metal and were very heavy to wear.

cloth from China that was bought in Russia. Fur was used to trim clothes for warmth and to make cloaks. Some cloaks were made of white fur on one side and black on the other.

Men wore white linen pants that were kept on at night. Over these, by day, they wore thick pants, and sometimes these were made with socks attached to the legs. It was fashionable to wear pants that were skintight. The long-sleeved shirt was made either of wool or linen. It had to have a narrow neck opening so as not to show the chest. Over the shirt a belted, knee-length *kyrtil*, or tunic, was worn. Usually it was blue, red or brown, but for important occasions it was scarlet, trimmed with fur and lace. The neck had to be high, for a woman could divorce her husband for showing his chest. Sometimes the tunic was worn tucked into the pants.

Women's clothes were simpler. A linen or silk vest was worn under a dress, or tunic. A woman's tunic reached to the ground. On top of it was an over-garment held up by shoulder straps and fastened with a pair of oval brooches. Women wore richly embroidered socks. At night, a white nightdress was worn. Unmarried girls and widows could let their hair hang loose, but married women wore a white linen headdress, which was sometimes embroidered with gold thread.

For special occasions, such as a feast or a visit to a king's court, men and women put on a robe called a *sloedur*. The woman's sloedur had a separate collar and was worn with a neckerchief round the throat. An Icelandic man named Egil was given a sloedur as a Yule gift by his friend. It was made of silk, heavily embroidered with gold thread and had gold buttons all down the front.

Cloaks were worn to keep warm out of doors. The most common kind, the *kapa*, had a hood and could be lined with fur. Only important men and women could wear a *möttul* (mantle). It was fastened at the neck with strings or a brooch and was often lined with fur. In Viking legend, a warrior called Ogmund was said to have made the kings he had conquered send him their

These silver rings were found at Sandby in Sweden. They may have been brought back by traders from Russia.

Right: Most Viking women wore a pair of large oval "tortoise" brooches, pinned on both sides of the chest. A necklace of brightly colored beads of crystal and glass would often be strung between them. The trefoil brooch in the center of the picture was worn in the middle of the chest.

Above: An ironing board and glass smoothing stone would have been a necessary piece of household equipment.

moustaches every year so that he could make a cloak with them.

Both men and women wore a hat for traveling. Men wore a wide-brimmed hat when they were working in the fields. They also wore a bowl-shaped woolly hat, stiffened inside with wooden rings, called a *skalhatt*. Wealthy men might own a Russian hat, bought from a merchant. It would be made from silk and trimmed with lace.

Jewelry was important to the Vikings, both as a form of wealth and also simply for decoration. Kings gave their followers gifts of gold bands for their hair, gold and silver belts, rings for their arms and necks and finger-rings. Men also wore splendid brooches made of gold and silver or sometimes bronze to fasten their cloaks, and their wives wore similar brooches to fasten strings of differently-colored glass beads across the chest.

Brooches were made in different shapes in clay molds. Some were round. Others were flat rings with a long pin. Oval "tortoise" brooches were raised and hollow and were worn in pairs. Trefoil brooches had three "arms". Women might also have chains hanging from their brooches. On the ends of the chains hung small articles that would be used everyday, such as a knife and a comb, scissors and needles, keys or possibly a purse.

Master Craftsmen

We think of the Vikings as mainly warriors and seafarers, but many of them were skilled craftsmen.

The Vikings' love of bright colors and ornaments was not limited to just their clothing and jewelry. Almost everything they used was covered with decoration. Gold and silver were highly valued. Most of it came from foreign coins which the craftsmen melted down. These metals were then shaped, by hammering and by casting, into wonderful ornaments.

Small ornaments were made by casting. A model of the ornament was made in wax or wood and the pattern carefully cut into it. This was covered in clay to make a mold. When the clay was hard the mold was cut in two and the model was taken out. Then the mold was put together again and hot metal was poured in. After it had cooled and hardened the craftsman would take the ornament out of the mold and polish the surface.

Brooches and other gold and silver ornaments were covered all over with patterns and borders of zigzags or stars. These were cut deeply into the metal by what is called "chip carving". Metalworkers copied this from wood-carvers. Chip carving helped a brooch to sparkle in the flickering firelight of a dark hall or in the sun out of doors. Chiefs and their wives liked their ornaments to glitter so that everyone noticed them.

Old craftsmen handed down their carefully guarded secrets to their young apprentices by word of mouth. One ancient skill was to make a pattern on a plain iron surface by inlaying wires of different metals. Valuable objects such as the blade of an axe, a sword-hilt or stirrups were decorated in this way. A pattern could be made with silver, bronze, copper or brass wires. Shallow grooves were cut on the iron surface to form a pattern. The wire was laid in the grooves and hammered down until it was fixed in place and the whole surface of the object was smooth.

THE GRIPPING BEAST

The Oseberg ship was made for a queen. Narrow bands of animal ornament were carved all along the stem and stern where they rose up out of the water. The curious pattern used in this type of animal art is known as the "Gripping Beast".

The Beast takes many different forms. It is not a real animal, but a mixture of lion, bear, dog and cat. Sometimes the Beast may have an almost human face. Its enormously long, thin body turns and twists and interlaces with itself. Its jaws and claws grip either its own body or that of another Beast intertwining with it. The hip and shoulder joints are often decorated with a spiral. Gripping Beasts appear everywhere. They were cast in metal and carved in wood and stone. They are even found writhing around the door posts of Viking churches.

Right: This iron axe blade from Mammen in Jutland is famous for its beautiful pattern of inlaid silver.

Runes were often carved inside the decorative body of a "beast". Runic stones like this one can still be seen today all over Sweden.

Sometimes wires were inlaid and then hammered so that they spread all over the iron and hid it. A pattern was then drawn on the new surface. Parts of the pattern were darkened with *niello*. Niello was a mixture of silver, lead, copper, sulfur and borax heated together. The ancestors of the Vikings had first learned the art of using niello from the ancient Romans.

Silver wire was used to decorate brooches and pendants with filigree ornament. Several thin wires were plaited together, or one wire was twisted to make a spiral. Then the ornamental wire was soldered around the edge of the brooch to make a border. Sometimes it was looped in patterns over the surface. The craftsmen had to know the different melting points of the metals they were using. Young metal-workers had a lot to learn.

Wood-carving was especially popular. Many everyday things were carved of wood. Shallow wooden dishes and troughs were shaped for preparing and serving food. Casks and buckets were made from staves, separate pieces of wood held together by metal bands and fitted into a base. Some wooden ladles were carved with a little foot so that they could stand upright on a table. Chairs, house beams and doorways were carved with Gripping Beast patterns. Few wooden things have been preserved, but the discovery of a Viking ship at Oseberg in Norway has given us a clear idea of the woodcarvers' skills.

On board the Oseberg ship were found sleighs and a splendid wagon. The sleigh bodies and wooden runners are carved all over with patterns and strange animal-like heads. The body of the wagon could be lifted off the wheels. It is covered with deeply carved animal patterns and scenes from legends. The body rested on a frame. Parts of this were difficult shapes to fill with ornament, but patterns were lightly drawn in the angles. The ends of the frame rise up in carved human heads that are very lifelike.

Some craftsmen were very clever stone-carvers. In Sweden, especially on the island of Gotland, hundreds of tall slabs were set upright in the ground. They are memorial stones to the dead. Some have runic inscriptions giving the names of the dead person and the relative who had the stone set up. The runes were often carved inside the long, writhing body of a Gripping Beast.

Above: This beautifully carved wagon was found on the Oseberg ship. It was probably only used on ceremonial occasions.

Below: Wooden posts on furniture, wagons and sleighs were beautifully shaped into strange animal heads. The heads were believed to frighten away evil spirits.

19

The Explosion

The Vikings' love of adventure and fighting, and the lack of good farmland at home, led them to explore and often raid the countries around them.

Just before AD 800, the Vikings began to overflow from Scandinavia like lava from an Icelandic volcano. They did not turn Europe into a huge empire as the Romans had done, but wandered far and wide in small independent groups. They were feared as brutal, heathen raiders, but they were also respected as brave and clever merchants. How were they able to travel so far, and why did so many of them leave their homelands to wander and often settle down in Britain, France, Russia or across the Atlantic?

It was their ships that made it possible for the Vikings to travel far and wide. Long before the Viking Age, the peoples of Scandinavia had been good boat-builders. They had always used rivers and seas as highways and were fearless sailors. When times were bad it was easy to raid richer neighbors, and also to go farther across the seas. The Vikings quickly came to know about the rich towns and the treasures stored in lonely monasteries in western Europe. Ships' crews also brought back reports about the wars going on in other countries. Wars meant that those countries were weak and open to attack. The Vikings had ships, courage and a love of adventure. It is not surprising that many of them sailed to look for treasure and land far away from home.

In search of land

It was new land, even more than loot, that the Vikings wanted. In Scandinavia, by the year 800, there was not enough good farming land for all the people. Raiding parties talked about the rich pastures of Ireland, the uninhabited islands in the Hebrides and the rolling hills of the north of England where few people lived. Norwegian chiefs set out for Scotland, Ireland and the north of England. Danes sailed over the North Sea to attack the Anglo-Saxon kingdoms. They won land in eastern England. The discovery of Iceland in particular encouraged the Scandinavians to leave their homelands. It is thought that over a period of about sixty years the population of Iceland grew to nearly 20,000 people.

In Sweden, the people were already trading in goods from other parts of Europe. Swedish chiefs moved into Finland and Russia in search of new trade routes. They set up colonies and demanded tribute of goods and coins from the native tribes. They used the tribute for trading. Norwegians, Swedes and Danes were all great traders, and this made many men travel. It was an exciting time, when men who dared could make their way west far over unknown seas, or south and east by land and river to a completely new world in the hot, dry countries of the Near East.

Above: Apart from a few Irish monks, Iceland was uninhabited when the Vikings first discovered it.

Ships were very important to the Vikings and they often included them in their carvings of legends and myths. This small sailing boat appears on a picture stone from Gotland in Sweden. The men are pulling on ropes to move the sail around to catch the wind.

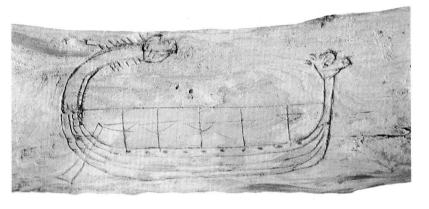

Left: The dragon-shaped heads of the Viking warships must have been a familiar sight to the man who carved this ship on a piece of wood.

Below: This anchor from a Viking ship looks very like the ones we use today. It is made of wood and iron and is almost 3 meters (9 feet) long.

Masters of the Sea

It was their ships that made the Vikings so powerful. They were faster and more seaworthy than any others that existed at that time.

We know more about the Vikings' ships than about the vessels of many other ancient peoples, because a number of their wooden ships have been found and are now in museums. Most old ships are left to rot on beaches or are wrecked. Luckily, there was a Viking belief that the spirits of important people had to sail to a land of the dead. Because of this a number of kings and queens were buried in their ships with all their belongings. In some places the ships were buried in damp clay and this has preserved the wood in perfect condition.

These small rowing boats were discovered alongside the Gokstad ship.

Ships of many sizes

The Vikings built different kinds of ships. For long voyages across the North Sea or across the Atlantic Ocean, they used the *hafskip*. This was like the ship that was found buried at Gokstad in Norway. It was over 23 meters (75 feet) long, and 5 meters (16 feet) broad. The stem, or prow, and the stern were high, and the sides swept down in a graceful curve to the center, where the mast was fitted into a solid block of oak. The ship was "clinker built". This means that the sides were built up by making the long planks, called *strakes*, overlap like the boards of a fence. The planks were thin and the whole ship was light. It weighed about 20 tons. Viking ships were made as light as possible so that they would float up and down on top of the great sea waves. This helped them to sail very fast. With a following wind a ship could sail over 193 kilometers (120 miles) in 24 hours.

Other ships were designed for sailing in sheltered coastal waters. Some were small sailing dinghies. Others would have been rowed. They had different names according to the number of oars they carried. Boats like this might have been used for making raids inland by rowing up rivers. A ship designed specially for carrying goods was called a *kaupskip* or *knorr*. This was wider than the hafskip and the sides were built higher to protect the cargo.

Viking kings had warships specially built for them. They did not need to be designed for long voyages far out to sea, because sea battles were fought only to defend their homelands or to raid their neighbors. There were different kinds of warships. The *skuta* was a small ship for raiding, with room for only fifteen men. The name of the *skeid* tells us that it was a "swift sailer". Larger warships were the *snekkja*, the *buza*, and the *dreki* (dragon), which had a carved dragon head on its prow.

It was the warships that had the most splendid dragon heads and stern posts. They were gilded so as to shine in the sun. The sides of the ship were painted dark blue, black and yellow, purple and gold, or red and white. The sails were especially fine. Some were of snow-white linen instead of the gray-white coarse wool of most vessels. They were embroidered, or had strips of colored cloth sewn on them in different designs.

All the large Viking ships were sailing craft. Oars were used only for getting in and out of harbor and for changing course quickly in a battle. When the ship was sailing, the oars were kept on the deck. The sail was square, about 90 square meters (107 square yards) in area. It hung from the *yard*, a pole about 11 meters (36 feet) long.

How a ship was built

The art of shipbuilding must have been handed down from person to person, for the Vikings did not write books of

instructions. The men who built the ships were very skilled and used special tools. They knew from experience exactly what kinds of wood and different materials were to be used in different parts of the ship. For the keel, a tall, straight oak tree was cut down and all the branches trimmed off. The stem- and stern-posts were joined to the ends of the keel. After the keel was laid, the planks, or strakes, were built up to form the sides of the ship. The planks were made by splitting tree trunks with wedges. They were fastened together with iron rivets. The joins between the planks were caulked (made watertight) with animal hair dipped in tar. The mast was made of pine. It was about 10 meters (33 feet) long and had to be very firmly held in place so that it did not blow down under the weight of the heavy sails.

Life on board

We think of the Vikings as always raiding other countries, but there were many men living among the islands around the coast of Scandinavia who raided the heavily laden ships belonging to their fellow countrymen. The sagas are full of stories about men whose possessions were stolen by pirate Vikings. When ships were anchored for the night, watchmen were always set on guard to warn of any attack. Even peaceful merchants and settlers had to carry weapons and be prepared to fight off pirates.

The Vikings did not go to sea in winter, but all the same they were often caught in terrible storms. One saga tells how a man named Fridthiof sailed from Norway to the Orkneys. He was caught in a snowstorm so thick that the men in the stem could not see those in the stern. They had to bale out the ship with wooden balers for a long time. Great waves dashed over the ship and swamped it and four men were washed overboard and drowned.

The people who left their farms in Norway to settle in other countries were very brave. Men, women and children set off with their animals in open boats without any protection in bad weather. The direct crossing to Iceland could take seven days with a following wind, but might be very much longer. Some captains went in stages. From Norway the ship would cross to the Shetlands, and there the people would be welcomed and spend some time ashore. Then they could move on to the Faeroes for another stay. When they finally came in sight of Iceland they would have a long sail along the south coast round to the natural harbors of the west.

It must have been very difficult living on board with the animals, but if the weather turned cold people could keep warm by huddling close to the animals.

Many families left Scandinavia to live and farm in new lands. Everything they might need for their new life had to be taken on board ship, including the farm animals. The colonists' ships were strong and seaworthy, but the journey must have been very crowded and uncomfortable.

The horses, sheep and cattle were very important passengers, for if they died on the journey there would be no stock for the new farms.

Viking ships were very shallow and could sail right up to a beach. They were so light that the crew could jump overboard and pull the ship up on shore for the night (or make a surprise attack on an enemy). Tree-trunk rollers were carried so that a beached ship could be pulled smoothly down to the sea on them if the tide had gone out.

A ship the size of the Gokstad vessel would have a crew of about 35 people on a long voyage. It was not possible to light a fire on board, so everyone had to eat cold food. The Vikings liked to run a ship ashore for the night whenever possible. Then they could use flint and steel to light a fire. They carried a big metal cauldron and could hang this over the fire on a collapsible tripod.

STEERING A COURSE

Viking ships were steered with an oar-like rudder, called the *styri*. It was fixed on the right-hand side of the ship, near the stern. This is how the right-hand side of a ship has come to be called the "starboard" side. The Vikings called it *stjornbordi*. The left-hand side was called *bakbordi*.

The captain of the ship, even if he was a king, would be the steersman. The deck at the stern was high, so that he could see right up the length of the ship and give orders. He was responsible for fixing a course.

Ships kept in sight of land as much as possible. In the open sea the helmsman would steer by the Sun or stars. He would hope to see the Sun in the middle of the day and could tell how far he had sailed to the north or south by its height above the horizon. Vikings were very experienced seamen. They were able to find their way across the Atlantic and tell others how they had done it.

Soup or porridge could be cooked for the whole crew. If they were at sea there was nothing hot, but still there was plenty of tasty food. The Vikings had bread that was hard and kept for a long time. With it they could eat cheese, smoked or salted meat and fish, and fish that had been dried on racks in the open air. This was tough to chew but delicious and very nourishing.

Food was prepared in wooden troughs and eaten from wooden platters. Casks of ale, beer or water were carried. Water was also carried in skin bags. If this ran short, rainwater could be collected in cloths strung between spars and crossbeams.

Every crew member kept his belongings in his heavy metal-bound sea chest. He sat on this to row and kept the key hidden. At night he slept in a leather sleeping bag.

During the day the crew would have to keep the ship's fittings in good repair as well as row or tend to the sails. However, when the ship was sailing before the wind there must have been plenty of time to relax and play gambling games with dice.

The Viking ship found buried at Gokstad, in Norway, is one of the most important burial finds yet discovered. From it, we have been able to understand how these ships were built.

A sword was a Viking's most prized possession. The iron hilts were often engraved and richly decorated with silver or gold.

Warriors and Weapons

A Viking was never very far away from his weapons. Even at home there were fights and family feuds.

Every able-bodied man had to be ready to fight. A farmer might have to defend his home and family against a raid, or a king or local chief might call up men to defend his land. There were no national armies. A man fought for his "lord", who rewarded him with gifts of gold ornaments, a sword or fine clothes, or even a ship.

The Vikings fought with swords and axes, spears and bows and arrows. A sword was a man's most precious possession and it was often beautifully decorated. A fine sword might be handed down from father to son. Many legends grew up about magic swords. Some were said to have been forged by dwarfs deep in the Earth. Others were the gift of Odin, the god of war. Some had magic runes engraved on them, or had been given the power to protect their owner through charms and spells chanted over them when they

were forged. In poems, swords were called "Odin's flame" or "The thorn of the shield". When a man wanted to show that he came in peace, his sword was bound into its scabbard with a strap called the *frithbönd*, "peace-band". This stopped him drawing his sword quickly and taking anyone by surprise.

The battle-ax, with its wide blade, was a favorite weapon of many Vikings. An Icelander, Skarphedinn, was never seen without his great axe "The ogress of war". Many were decorated with patterns inlaid on the blade. Poetic names for the axe were "The witch of the helmet" and "The fiend of the shield", because an ax could cut through these at a stroke.

There were different kinds of spears depending on how they were to be used. Some were for throwing and others for stabbing at close quarters. Spear-shafts were made of ash wood. They were 3 centimeters (1 inch) thick and over 3 meters (10 feet) long. Spearheads might be inlaid with patterns in gold and silver. Throwing spears had a mark on the shaft so that a man could quickly find the right place to hold the spear in the heat of battle. Spears were called "The serpent of blood", or "The flying dragon of the wound".

This chess piece comes from the Hebrides. It was carved in the 12th century, and shows that the ferocious Viking warriors who had taken over the islands many years before were still clearly remembered by the people who lived on the islands.

THE WAR ARROW
If a king had to raise an army quickly he would send out the war arrow. When the arrow was brought to a house the owner and all available men over 15 years old had to take their weapons and go to the meeting place. Even guests and thralls had to go. The arrow would then be carried on to the next homestead. If the householder was a woman who was running her own estate, she had to provide men from her household if she could. If not, she had to provide a ship and food. Anyone who did not obey the call of the war arrow was outlawed.

A bow was nearly 2 meters (6 feet) long. Four rows of feathers were tied on to the arrows with tarry thread. The arrow-head had barbs of bone or iron. There were legends about the famous Gusi arrows given to the hero Orvar-Odd by his father. The feathers were gilded and the arrows flew on and off the bowstring by themselves. They never missed their target and they always came back.

Kings and jarls sometimes wore iron helmets, but these were expensive and rare. A helmet often had a nose-guard attached to it. A king's helmet would be gilded so that his men could see where he was in battle. A mailcoat was also expensive to buy and would only have been worn by wealthy men.

Shields were carried in defense against spears and arrows. They were round and were made of wood, with a metal rim. The center was made of iron or bronze with a handle on the inside. Shields were colored red, brown, white or blue. Some had scenes from legends painted on them. A white shield was held up as a signal for a parley, or was hoisted to the masthead as a sign of surrender in a sea battle. A red shield on the masthead was a declaration of war.

Above: Most Viking soldiers carried a spear, although not all of them would be as richly decorated as the one shown here.

This ornate helmet was found in a grave at Vendel in Sweden. It was made before the Viking Age, but it is possible that parts of this style were still being copied in Viking times.

THE MAGIC RAVEN STANDARD

Sigurd, Jarl of Orkney, was worried because he was going to fight against an enemy whose army was seven times as large as his own. His mother said scornfully that it was better for him to die with honor than to live with the shame of being a coward. However, she gave him a magic flag with a raven embroidered on it. The raven was a bird associated with the war god Odin. When the wind blew the raven seemed to spread his wings. The flag brought victory to the leader of the army who used it, but the man who carried it would always die. Sigurd gained many victories with his magic standard, until a battle in 1014, when one standard-bearer after another was cut down. Sigurd was forced to carry the raven himself and paid the penalty.

Men went into battle after a good meal and with their hair washed and combed. They would meet together beforehand so that their leader could tell them his battle plans and what the war cry was. He would say where his standard would be set up, and who would fight around the standards of the different chiefs.

would fight hard to defend the others.

One king placed groups of friends and kinsmen together, so that each Also, they would know one another by sight. In an army that was made up of people from different regions, it was hard in battle to know who was a friend and who an enemy. Sometimes men had signs painted on their shields and helmets.

Battle began when horns were blown and an arrow or spear was sent high in the air over the opposing army. Afterwards, the spoils were divided according to the rank of each chief and the number of men he had brought to the battle.

Merchants and Adventurers

The trade routes to the east and the new lands far to the west offered wealth and adventure to those who had the courage to reach them.

These silver Arabian coins were brought to Scandinavia by traders from the East. The coins themselves had little value to the Vikings; it was the metal they were made of that was important.

Across the Baltic from Sweden to the east lie the Gulf of Finland and Lake Ladoga. About AD 850, colonists from Sweden settled at Staraja Ladoga, among the Finns. Many of them took land round about for farming. It was not long before Swedish adventurers went exploring down the great rivers leading into the heart of Russia.

By the 10th century AD, they had established two important trade routes to rich markets. One went down the River Dnieper to reach Constantinople in the south. The other went east, along the River Volga to Bulghar, where the Vikings met traders from the Near East and China.

The way to the east
A merchant traveling to Constantinople would make his way by boat from Staraja Ladoga to Novgorod and Kiev.

This statue of Buddha was found at Helgo in Sweden. It was buried in about the 8th century, and shows that even before the Viking Age, Swedish traders had found their way to the East.

These were two Swedish colonies whose inhabitants were called *Rus*. This name probably came from the Finnish word *Ruotsi*, meaning Sweden. Originally the name "Rus" was used to describe the Swedes in Russia, but it gradually spread far and wide as the name, not only for all Scandinavians in Russia, but also for the native Slavs over whom they ruled.

Traders in Kiev who were going to Constantinople would gather their goods together between November and April. Every June, a fleet of small boats left Kiev. The traders had to be certain of returning before the rivers froze in winter. Ten days after leaving Kiev, the party would reach the terrible Dnieper rapids. There were seven of these, and they were given names by the Vikings, like "The Gulper" and "The Everfierce", to describe their dangers. In June, the river level was still high after the spring floods. Then it was possible to sail through the rapids.

Beyond the rapids there was an island in the middle of the river, where the travelers rested and made thankful sacrifices at a great oak tree. At last, they came to the Black Sea and sailed across to the great city of Constantinople. This was the largest city the Vikings had ever seen and they called it Mikligard, the "Great City".

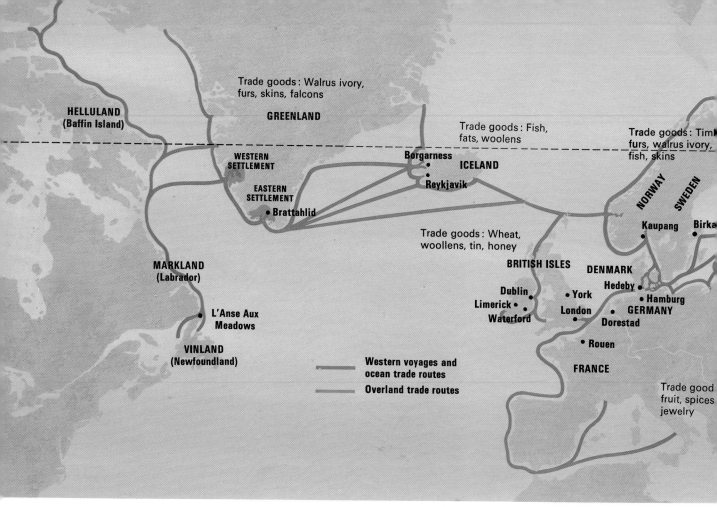

Trade goods: Walrus ivory, furs, skins, falcons

HELLULAND
(Baffin Island)

GREENLAND

Trade goods: Fish, fats, woolens

Trade goods: Tim[
furs, walrus ivory,
fish, skins

**WESTERN
SETTLEMENT**

Borgarness

ICELAND

Reykjavik

**EASTERN
SETTLEMENT**

Brattahlid

NORWAY **SWEDEN**

Kaupang Birka

MARKLAND
(Labrador)

Trade goods: Wheat,
woollens, tin, honey

BRITISH ISLES

DENMARK

L'Anse Aux
Meadows

Hedeby

Dublin York Hamburg

Limerick London **GERMANY**

VINLAND
(Newfoundland)

Waterford Dorestad

Rouen

FRANCE

—— Western voyages and
ocean trade routes

—— Overland trade routes

Trade good[
fruit, spices
jewelry

THE VARANGIAN GUARDS

The name of these famous warriors probably comes from the word *var,* meaning "pledge". It was used of men who swore an oath to stay together and to be loyal to the group. The Varangians were paid soldiers from different parts of Scandinavia who agreed to fight for the Rus princes of Novgorod and Kiev.

They had many privileges. Prince Vladimir of Kiev consulted them about affairs of state, as well as taking their advice on how to plan his wars. However, many of his guards became angry when they did not get paid for their services, and they went off to serve the Emperor at Constantinople. In the 10th century, the Varangians fought for the Emperor in Crete, South Italy, Iraq and Romania. About the year 1000 they formed the Emperor's personal guard.

To Bulghar and Baghdad

The journey down the Volga to Bulghar was easier than traveling down the Dnieper. When merchants arrived at Bulghar they were allowed to build wooden huts where they could live and trade. In return, they had to hand over one out of every ten of their slaves to the king of the Bulghars. Bulghar must have been a very exciting place. Blonde Swedes would come face to face with swarthy Arab traders with bags of silver coins to spend.

From Bulghar, a Swedish merchant could return home to spend his silver Arabian coins at Birka. The more adventurous sailed on down the Volga to the Caspian Sea. They crossed the Caspian and went on camels over the deserts to Baghdad. Some of them even took to wearing the baggy eastern trousers. What tales they would have to tell when they returned to the cold north with their Arabian silver, Persian glassware, strange spices and embroidered Indian purses.

The Vikings in the west

It was not only the merchants who went exploring far away from home. Other Viking people were also looking for new lands in the west. A Norwegian, called Eirik the Red, was outlawed from Norway for killing a man and went to Iceland. When he also killed men there he was banished for three years. He decided to try to find a new land to the west, that had been sighted by another Norwegian when he had been driven off course by a storm some 50 years before.

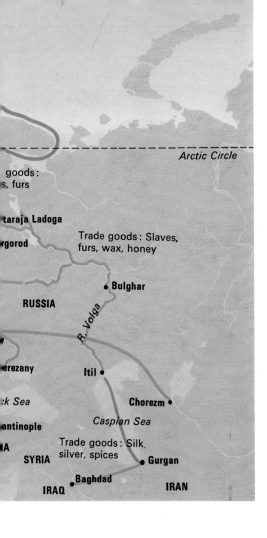

goods:
s, furs

taraja **Ladoga**

'gorod

Trade goods: Slaves,
furs, wax, honey

• **Bulghar**

RUSSIA

R. Volga

erezany

Itil •

:k Sea

Chorezm •

Caspian Sea

antinople

IA

SYRIA

Trade goods: Silk,
silver, spices

• **Gurgan**

• **Baghdad**

IRAQ

IRAN

Arctic Circle

Below: The site of Eirik the Red's
settlement at Brattahlid in Greenland. From
here, Leif Eiriksson set out to find America.

In the year 982, Eirik the Red sailed from Borgarness in western Iceland, to the icy east coast of Greenland. He could not farm there, so he went on to find good land on the west coast where he stayed during his exile. Cattle could graze on the grassy slopes, and there were foxes, polar bears, caribou and seals to hunt for their meat and fur or skin. Birds could be caught with snares, and the fishing was good. As soon as he could, Eirik went back to Iceland and brought about 450 people back with him to the country he had named "Greenland". The newcomers lived in farms around two settlements and agreed on laws that everyone should obey. They had plenty of meat, but they had to import nearly all the grain they needed, as well as iron tools and weapons and timber for building.

In 986, an Icelander called Bjarni Herjolfsson was driven off course by a storm on his way to Greenland. He was lost in a fog for some days before the weather cleared and he saw a coast with low hills covered with trees. He did not know where he was, but he knew it could not be mountainous, treeless Greenland. He sailed along the coast for two days without landing (later Vikings thought this was very cowardly of him) and then managed to find his way to Greenland. He had become the first European to see North America.

"Land of Pastures"

It was not for another 15 years that anyone else looked for this new land, but Bjarni's voyage was not forgotten. When Leif, son of Eirik the Red, decided to sail west to settle he bought Bjarni's ship and took some of his crew with him. Leif was bolder than Bjarni. He landed in several places, first of all on the southern part of Baffin Island. He called this Helluland, "Flat Stone Land", as it was mountainous and icy with no grass. He then sailed south to Labrador, with its shelving beaches of white sand and forests of useful timber. He called this Markland, "Wood Land". Leif and his crew spent the winter on the north coast of Newfoundland, which he named Vinland, meaning "Land of Pastures".

In the summer he sailed back to Greenland to tell of the beautiful country he had discovered, but as his father had died Leif had to stay in Greenland. After this, in about AD 1007, Eirik's daughter Gudrid and her husband Thorfinn Karlsefni tried to settle in Vinland. The Indians they met were hostile and the colonists quarreled among themselves. After three winters they returned to Greenland.

Sagas tell many details about the Viking exploration of eastern North America, but it seems that there was never a successful Viking colony in North America. The trees there were useful to the people of Greenland, and a few traders went there for timber and furs until 1347, but the settlement in Greenland was itself doomed to failure. The people there were too far from Norway to survive without supplies of imported goods and food. The climate became colder and pack ice began to close their harbors. Eskimos, who did not mind the cold, began to attack the settlements, and all the colonists either perished or left.

Raiders and Settlers

The Vikings were seen as bloodthirsty heathens, but many of them became peaceful settlers.

Very few people in western Europe could write at the time of the Viking Age, so the task of writing about the events of the time was done by Christian monks. Their accounts of Viking raids would make us think that the Vikings descended like wolves on a helpless, peaceful Europe.

However, when we really study all the histories written in monasteries during the Viking Age, we can see a different picture. The Vikings did not come with a huge army to wage war. Some bands were only one or two ships' crews, about 60 men, although a large raiding party might be up to 400 strong. Also, the Vikings raided in lands where wars were already being fought. Ireland and England were divided into small kingdoms which battled amongst themselves, and in France in the 8th century, the Emperor Charlemagne fought brutal wars against the Saxons of north Germany for 30 years.

Why then did the monk historians in western Europe see the Viking raids as so much more terrible? The first reason is that the Vikings appeared suddenly, without warning, and people had no time to band together and fight. The second reason is that the heathen Vikings dared to demand tribute money from the monks. In wars between Christian kings, churches and monasteries were left in peace, and the monks who wrote about them were never in danger.

Vikings in the British Isles

The Vikings began to raid in Britain before AD 800. The first attack we know of was when a royal official was killed on the south coast of England in 789. Then, in 793, the lonely monastery at Lindisfarne in Northumbria was sacked and looted. After this many Viking bands came raiding.

A number of Vikings had already settled peacefully in the Hebrides Islands off the coast of Scotland, and in the Isle of Man. Later, in about 860, Norwegians settled in the Shetlands and the Orkneys. From the Hebrides, they went raiding in Ireland and a group of Norwegians settled there along the east and south coasts. After about the year 850, the Danes also raided in Ireland. They attacked both Irish and Norwegian settlements.

In 876, Norwegians settled in the English city of York and set up their own kingdom there. They ruled over the English state of Northumbria. Meanwhile, the Danes made many attacks in the south of England. King Alfred the Great of Wessex led his people against them, and it was only

Scenes from the Bayeux tapestry show the invasion of England by a Norman fleet. The battle that followed put a 'Viking' king on the English throne.

Ruins of Viking long houses on the Orkney Islands. From here, the Vikings could raid the coast of Scotland.

his courage and skill that stopped the whole of England becoming a Scandinavian land.

In the year 886, King Alfred won a victory over a Danish leader, Guthrum. Guthrum agreed to be baptized and became a Christian with all his followers. Guthrum and Alfred made a treaty. The Danes were allowed to settle in eastern England. This area became known as the 'Danelaw', and both Englishmen and Danes lived peacefully there as farmers.

Vikings in France
The Vikings first came to mainland Europe as peaceful traders. It was not until the 9th century that they began to raid there. In 834 they plundered the rich undefended market town of Dorestad on the Rhine. After this, fleets of ships rowed up the rivers to attack inland towns such as Rouen in France, another great trading centre.

France suffered greatly from Viking attacks. In 911, the Franks allowed a chief called Rollo to settle with his followers in Normandy. The Franks hoped that if they gave Rollo land he would help them to fight off other Vikings.

Normandy was good land for farming. Rollo gave out land to his chief followers, and they shared it among their own men. Rollo was a wise ruler. He made Normandy a peaceful land with well-defended towns. He realized that it would be better for his people to learn the ways of the Franks than to carry on their Viking traditions. This made Normandy very different from the Danelaw in England, where the laws and customs were still Danish.

There were very few Viking women in Normandy and Rollo's men married Frankish women who were Christian. Their children grew up more Frankish than Viking. Rollo himself was baptized and Normandy became a Christian country. Even the Scandinavian language disappeared and the Normans began to speak a form of French.

Like their Viking ancestors, the Normans were good fighters. In the 11th century they sent an expedition to the Mediterranean and captured the island of Sicily. Then, in 1066, the Norman Duke William invaded England. He won a victory over the Saxon King Harold at the Battle of Hastings, and the Norman Duke became the King of England.

The Colony in Iceland

The discovery of Iceland offered a golden opportunity to the land-hungry Vikings. Every available strip of grassland was soon claimed by settlers.

CLAIMING LAND

When a new settler sighted land, he would have the carved wooden "high seat pillars" he had brought from his old home thrown overboard. He believed that the god Thor would bring them ashore at the place where he was to build his farm. The family would land and men would ride out to look for the high seat pillars. At last they would be found. The new settler would go to the place and light a fire. The first settlers took huge amounts of land, which they then divided amongst their followers. Then in the year 930, a law was passed to limit the amount of land each new settler could claim. A man could claim as much land as he could carry a burning torch around in one day.

Iceland was given its name by a Norwegian who went looking for land to settle in the northwest. He climbed a mountain ridge and looked over the top at a bay filled with thick ice. The sight made him change his mind about farming in *Island*, "Ice-land". Iceland is a little larger than Ireland and although one-eighth of the land is covered by ice sheets, the weather is not terribly cold because the shores of Iceland are warmed by the Gulf Stream. However, in winter the sea around it is deadly cold. The rigging of a ship can get so heavy with ice that the vessel will overturn and sink.

Then too, there are dangers on the land. Iceland has active volcanoes. Whole districts have been covered with fast flowing lava. Huge areas far away from erupting volcanoes can be coated with ash. Ash kills the grass so that there is no pasture for animals. When this happened to the Viking settlements the animals died of starvation, and then their owners died too.

steam rising from the many hot springs along the shore. He called the place Reykjavik, which means "Smoke Bay", and settled there. Other settlers soon followed Ingolf.

The Althing

The chief man in a group of settlers looked after his followers. He was known as the *gothi*. At first, the chiefs were independent rulers of Iceland, which was small enough for people to know one another wherever they lived. After a time, the chiefs realized that the new country needed laws. They sent a respected man, Ulfljot, to Norway to study the laws there and to make a new code of laws for Iceland.

The chiefs then decided to appoint a Lawspeaker. He would preside over a national assembly, the *Althing*, which all free men could attend. Grim, Ulfljot's foster-brother, was sent all over Iceland to find a place where thousands of people could gather together. He chose a wide, flat stretch of grass beside a lake at Oxara, the "Axe-river". This is now called Thingvellir. On one side the grass slopes up the side of a natural rocky gorge that runs across the countryside. A small hillock in front of the gorge was named "The Hill of Laws". On it, every year, the Lawspeaker stood and declaimed one-third of the laws of Iceland. He knew all the laws by heart. His voice echoed back from the large wall of rock behind him and could be heard for a great distance.

From the beginning, the Icelanders had a great sense of law and order, but the laws and the Althing did not make Iceland a peaceful country. Many Vikings who went to Iceland were violent men who loved to fight. The decisions of the law courts were not supported by a police force. There was no way of making people obey the law if it did not suit them. The only thing that did help to make people keep the laws was public opinion. Even violent men cared what people thought about them, and how they would be remembered in sagas after their death.

The Althing was one of the oldest parliaments. It was first held in the year 930, and then every year for two weeks in midsummer. People gathered from all over Iceland. They brought their lawsuits to be judged, but they also came to meet friends, arrange marriages and to trade with one another.

However, in spite of the dangers, life was easier for the Vikings in Iceland than at home in Norway where there were far too many people trying to fish and farm. Round the coasts there was rich grass for cattle. Sheep could graze on upland heaths. There was little arable soil, but some barley could be grown. In the rivers were many trout and salmon, and there were cod and herring in the sea. Great flocks of seabirds nested on the cliffs, and their eggs could be collected for food.

Iceland was first sighted about AD 860, by men on ships that were blown off course by storms. The first settler was Ingolf Arnason. In 874, he came to a promontory now called Ingolf's Head in southeast Iceland. He threw his high seat pillars overboard when he first saw land. Then he sent thralls out to look for them. They were found washed up in a bay in the southwest of Iceland. Ingolf looked at the clouds of

Detail from a church tapestry showing the three gods, Odin, Thor and Frey.

World of the Gods

Worship of the gods was a very practical thing. Sacrifices were made to them, but in return they were expected to give victory in battle and good crops.

The Vikings worshiped many gods and goddesses. They believed there were two families of gods, the Asar and the Vanir. At one time the two families had been at war. The most important Asar gods were Odin and his wife Frigg; Thor the thundergod; Tyr, a god of war; Odin's son Baldr; and Loki, who was a troublemaker. The Vanir gods were Mimir, Niord and his son and daughter, Frey and Freyja. Freyja was always attended by cats.

The one-eyed Odin was the chief of the gods, and the most mysterious god of all. He was concerned with magic and the dead. Kings and warriors sacrificed to him because he could grant them victory in war. The sacrifices sometimes involved terrible rites when men and horses were killed with spears and hung on trees. Odin was also very wise. He had given one of his eyes to get a drink from Mimir's Well of Knowledge beneath Yggdrasil's Ash Tree. He had two ravens, Hugin and Mugin ("Thought" and "Memory"). Every day at dawn he sent them out to fly all over the world. Each night they flew back and told him everything that had happened that day.

Sometimes Odin roamed the world of men as Grim, an old man in a wide-brimmed hat and cloak. There were tales in the sagas of his visits to kings who had become Christian, to try to persuade them to worship him again.

Festivals and sacrifices

There were three important festivals in the Viking year. At Vetrarblot, in mid-October, animals were sacrificed for a good winter. At Jolablot (Yule) in mid-January, sacrifices were offered for good crops in the coming season. At Sigrblot, in April, sacrifices were

This small statue is thought to represent the god Odin. Odin was not a popular god, but he was very powerful.

YGGDRASIL'S ASH TREE

The Vikings had a myth about a huge world tree called Yggdrasil's Ash. Its branches held up the sky. Beneath the tree was Asgarth, the home of the gods. Long roots spread out from the base of the trunk. One covered Midgarth, the world of men. Another root covered the realm of the terrible Frost Giants. A third root covered Hel, the world of the dead. Also among the roots were two wells. A drink of water from the well of the wise god Mimir gave knowledge. Beside the other well, the Well of Fate, lived the three Norns. They were called Past, Present and Future. They wove a cloth. Every thread represented the life of a person. When they cut a thread that person died.

Left: A Viking burial site. Stones have been placed around each grave to give it the outline of a ship. This was to help the spirits of the dead people to sail to the land of the dead.

went to a hell where they were punished. Some Vikings thought that the dead person's spirit sailed to a new life, where the things used on Earth would still be needed. Sometimes kings and queens were buried in a ship with many of their possessions, and even the graves of many ordinary people had stones placed around them in the outline of a ship. There was also a belief that the dead came to life inside the burial mound over their grave. Women were buried with their jewelry and tools and men with their weapons. A slave girl might also be killed so that she could go with her master to serve him.

Warriors who had died bravely in battle were believed to go to Odin's paradise, which was a huge hall called Valhalla. Here they would be welcomed and would sit and feast until the end of the world.

offered for victory in war. Fighting took place in summer.

At the sacrifices, animals and sometimes men were killed. Blood was sprinkled on the wall of the hall and on the worshipers. Horsemeat was cooked in a great cauldron for a feast, and ale was drunk from great bowls that were passed around. Bowls of ale were drunk in the name of different gods, and men made vows over the bowls before they drank. Sometimes the animal given to a god did not have to be killed. An Icelander, Hrafnkell, told everyone that he was giving half of all his best possessions to Frey. His favorite horse was called Freyfaxi after the god. It had a dark stripe along its back. Hrafnkell shared the horse with Frey, but he could still go on riding it.

Life after death

The Vikings did not believe that the spirits of good people always went to a heaven and that the spirits of bad people

THE END OF THE WORLD

The Vikings believed that one day the world would come to a terrible end. This was Ragnarök, the "Doom of the Gods". They would be killed by their enemies the Giants and by monster animals. Ragnarök would come after three years of continuous winter and three years of continuous war. The Sun and Moon would be swallowed by huge wolves. Midgarthsorm, a serpent coiled round the Earth, would rise from the sea, spitting out poison. Giants would ride against Asgarth, the home of the gods.

Heimdall, the watchman, lived on Bifrost, the rainbow bridge leading to Asgarth. When he saw the Giants coming he would call out the warriors who were feasting in Valhalla.

All the gods would die in the attack. Odin would be swallowed by the terrible wolf Fenrir. Thor would fight the dreaded serpent Midgarthsorm. He would kill it but would die from its venom. Frey would be killed by Surt the Fire Giant, whose sword flashed brighter than the Sun. In the end, the stars would fall from the sky and the Earth would sink into the sea. But all would not be lost. A few of the sons of the old gods and of men would survive with their wives, to people a new and better world that would rise out of the waters.

The Battle for Christianity

For many years the Viking people were divided between the old religion and the new.

For much of the Viking Age the people of Scandinavia would not give up worshiping the old gods. Missionaries from England and Germany came to Denmark and Sweden, but many went home discouraged or were expelled. Missionaries were very brave. They could only work in a country if they had the favor of the king. Gradually, kings saw that becoming Christian would be useful in their dealings with the powerful Christian rulers of the rest of Europe. Harald Blue-tooth, king of Denmark, became Christian in about 960. He set up a great stone at Jelling. The runic inscription says that he was "that Harald who made all the Danes Christian".

Conversion was more difficult in Norway, which was farther from Christian lands. Hakon the Good became Christian as a child when he was brought up at the court of King Athelstan in England. He returned to Norway in 934 as king. He lost the support of the people because he refused to eat horsemeat and to sacrifice to the gods at the great festivals. People believed this would bring bad seasons, and Hakon lost the throne.

In 995, Olaf Tryggvason became king of Norway. He went round the country threatening to put people to death if they would not be baptized. Many Icelanders visited Olaf's court in Norway. They found that they were expected to become Christian. Olaf even kept four important young men as hostages, while two of their friends, Gizur and Hjalti, went back to Iceland to try to make the country Christian.

In the year 1000, the two men spoke at the Althing and proposed that everyone should be baptized. This caused an uproar. Icelanders at this time thought that if there was a Christian in the family it was a stain on the family

Olaf's saga gives an exciting account of the Battle of Svold. Olaf's friends begged him to run for home because his enemies had a larger fleet, but Olaf had never avoided a fight. Olaf was in his famous ship the "Long Serpent", which had a gilded dragon head at the prow. He fought amongst his men with a bow and a spear until the battle was lost and he leaped into the sea.

honor. At the Althing, people divided into two groups. Each elected a Lawspeaker and said that the other was outlawed. In the end, everyone agreed to act on the advice of Thorgeir, the respected heathen Lawspeaker.

It was a great responsibility. Thorgeir went into his tent for a day and a night, with a cloak wrapped round his head so he could think in peace. He realized that Iceland could not resist the will of Olaf, as Icelanders had to go to Norway to trade. He thought out a good way to make the country Christian without forbidding the worship of the old gods all at once. He proposed that all Icelanders should be baptized and be officially Christians, but that people could go on sacrificing to the gods and eating horsemeat, so long as they were not seen doing it. If they did it openly they could be punished.

The Battle of Svold

Although Olaf Tryggvason brought about the conversion of Iceland, in Norway the people revolted against him, and he was killed in a great sea battle in AD 1000. The battle took place off an island called Svold. King Olaf had been to Poland to claim some land that his wife owned there. His enemies, the kings of Denmark and Sweden, and an exiled Norwegian chief, Jarl Eirik, met with their fleets to ambush Olaf who was sailing home with only a few ships.

At first Olaf's men successfully beat off the enemy ships that grappled on to them. Then his men grew tired and began to give way. The survivors gathered round the King. Olaf saw that all was lost. He leaped from the ship into the sea. His body was never found, and there were many tales that he had been picked up by a ship and carried off to Poland. As his saga says, "Be that as it may, King Olaf never again returned to his kingdom in Norway".

It was only in the reign of Olaf the Holy (1014-1030) that English and German missionaries succeeded in making Norway a Christian country. In Sweden, the worship of Odin went on even longer. Although a Swedish king became Christian in 1008, the famous heathen temple at Uppsala was not destroyed until late in the 12th century.

Legends, Poetry and Magic

Bravery and loyalty were much admired by the Vikings. They loved to tell stories and poems of great deeds and famous warriors.

The Icelandic sagas were not written down until the Middle Ages. This illustration comes from a page in the "Flateyarbok," which contains the stories of the lives of the kings of Norway. The panel in the center shows Olaf Tryggvason, the Norwegian king who converted the Icelanders to Christianity.

In the evenings after the main meal of the day, a Viking household settled down to drinking and entertainment. A storyteller might tell a saga about the life of a king or of the deeds of a famous family. A *skald*, a traveling poet, might recite verses about the gods or the heroes of old. He may even have made up a new poem, praising the chief or king he was visiting.

Vikings had no pens or paper. They used a runic alphabet, and they carved the letters on wood or stone. This took a long time. Poems and stories were not written down in runes. They were passed down by word of mouth from the older poets and storytellers to the young men. Some of the poems had been made up in the 6th century, long before the Viking Age. They were told over and over again and were not forgotten.

Tales of heroes and magic

The word *saga* means "spoken". Sagas were stories learned by heart and told on winter evenings. They were all composed in Iceland. Some of the settlers in Iceland had lived for a time in Ireland. The art of storytelling was very old among the Irish Celts and the Vikings learned it from them.

Icelanders composed sagas about the lives of the kings of Norway. One storyteller was staying at the court of King Harald Hardrada. One day the King noticed that the storyteller was looking worried. When he asked why, the Icelander said that he had only one saga left to tell. That was the saga of the journey of King Harald himself to the south, and he did not dare to tell that in front of the King. The King said that he was to be brave and tell part of the saga every night during the Yule festival. He would have to wait until he had finished before the King would let him know what he thought of it. The King listened to an instalment of the saga on each of the 12 nights of Yule. At the end, he rewarded the nervous storyteller with goods for trading. The skald said that he had learned the saga, a little every year, at the Althing in Iceland from a famous saga-teller, known to King Harald.

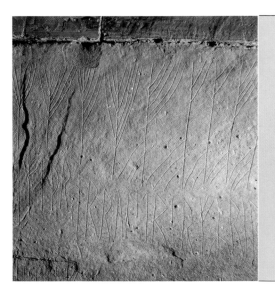

The sagas are not historical records. They were stories told to entertain people and not everything described in them really happened. For example, some people in the sagas were said to have had "second sight". This meant that they had the power to foretell the future and to see supernatural beings that were invisible to ordinary people. The Vikings believed that everyone had a *fylgja*, an animal spirit that went about with them. One day an old man laughed when a little boy ran into the hall and fell over. The boy asked why it was funny. The old man said that the boy's fylgja was a polar bear cub. It came into the hall ahead of him and stopped when it saw the old man. The boy came behind and fell over it.

The Vikings also believed in witches and wizards. Some were good and some bad. A good witch was called a *spa-kona*, a "wise-woman". Farmers used to invite a spa-kona to a feast to ask her when a bad season would end, and to foretell the future. She stood on a platform to perform her magic, and girls had to stand around it singing ancient songs. This summoned up the spirits who would reveal the future to her.

In the sagas, wizards often caused storms at sea so that men who were pursuing them to put them to death would lose their way. One wizard wrapped a goatskin round his head and said "Become mist and fog, become fright and wonder to those that seek you". Wizards could also bring good weather to their friends.

Poetry in everyday use
Although many people think of the Vikings only as bloodthirsty pirates, they had a great love of poetry. Many of them could compose complicated verses in their heads, to describe unusual events that had happened. Viking poetry did not rhyme, but several words within the lines had to begin with the same letter.

There was also a poetic language. Many everyday things had an elaborate name, a *kenning*, in a poem. Every Viking knew that "the fire of the arm" meant gold (gold was used for armlets that gleamed like flames in the sun), or that "The hawk's land" meant the arm, where a man's hawk sat.

Skalds were highly respected by everyone, and particularly by kings, because their poems could either make a king's name famous after his death, or ridiculous. A clever poet could grow rich by staying at a king's court and composing poems in praise of the king's courage. These poems were called *drapas*. If the king was pleased with the poem he would reward the poet with gifts. Two kings promised the same skald a reward for the drapas he had composed for them. The two kings were at war. The skald told them that the reward he wanted was that they should make peace and the kings agreed.

Some skalds even went into battle with a king. Before the fighting began the skald would recite heroic poetry to inspire the men to fight as bravely as the heroes of old. The skald would stay beside the king during the fighting so that if the king died he could give a blow by blow account of his last battle.

KENNINGS

A battle
The song of the spears.
The weapon's Thing (council).

A warrior
The feeder of the wolf.
The diminisher of peace.

A horse
The ship of the ground.
The deer of the saddle.

Blood
The dew of the sword.
The ale of the wolf.

Fire
The thief of the house.
The brother of the wind.

A SKALD'S REWARD

Skalds traveled everywhere, making up poems in praise of chiefs or kings they were visiting. They would recite the *drapa* in front of the king and his warband. If the king enjoyed the poem he would reward the skald with rich gifts and invite him to stay for the winter.

The skald Gunnlaug Serpent's Tongue visited Sihtric Silkybeard in Dublin. Sihtric had only just become king and this was the first time a poet had made up a drapa for him.

After he had finished the drapa, Gunnlaug waited hopefully for his reward. Sihtric's men applauded wildly. The young king whispered to his treasurer, asking him anxiously whether he should give the poet two merchant ships. The treasurer was horrified and said that was far too much. Most kings only gave an armlet or a sword. Sihtric was very pleased and proud. He gave Gunnlaug a new suit of clothes, a fur cloak and a gold ring of great value.

A scene from a wood-carving of the story of the hero Sigurd the Volsung. Sigurd slew the dragon Fafnir. Here, he is roasting the dragon's heart. He accidentally tasted its blood and was then able to understand the language of some kinds of birds. The birds told him to take the dragon's gold.

The Legacy

Although the Viking Age lasted for only 300 years, we still find traces of it in our modern world.

In the Viking Age, people of Scandinavian origin spread far and wide into distant lands. They often married native women, who bore them children of mixed blood. Many countries in Europe, from Brittany and Russia to Sicily in the south, have some Viking ancestors among their populations. There is a high proportion of Viking blood in the Normans, the Scots and the people of north and eastern England. In fact, many of the people who read this book could be the descendants of the far-traveled warriors and traders of the Viking world.

In the lands once occupied by Viking settlers, one legacy that remains is the Scandinavian language. In Orkney and Shetland people now speak Gaelic and English, but even until the 18th century, they spoke Scandinavian tongues called "Norn" We can trace many English words back to the Vikings. Our word "bylaw", from the Viking word *by* for "village", means a local, not a national

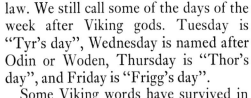

Part of a Viking tomb that was found in St Paul's churchyard in London.

The Oseberg ship. The splendid Viking ships that were once used for royal burials are today carefully preserved in special museums.

law. We still call some of the days of the week after Viking gods. Tuesday is "Tyr's day", Wednesday is named after Odin or Woden, Thursday is "Thor's day", and Friday is "Frigg's day".

Some Viking words have survived in France too. The French word for porpoise is *marsouin*. This comes from the Viking word *marsvin*, meaning "sea-swine"

Everywhere the Vikings settled they introduced coinage, which made trade easier, and they founded towns for trading. In England they helped London and York to become important centers. In Ireland they founded Dublin and other towns and established the busy sea routes between Ireland and the English ports of Chester and Bristol. These became very important later, in the Middle Ages.

Among the few traces of Vikings in Wales are the names that they gave to staging posts and to prominent places that they used for fixing their course when they were on the Irish Sea. Among these are Bardsey Island, Orme's Head, Skokholm, and Fishguard (from *fiskrgarthr*, 'fishyard'). Also, the Viking love of law and lawsuits has had a lasting effect on our laws. The Vikings were the first to use a jury of 12 ordinary people to decide if someone was guilty or not at a lawsuit.

Glossary

Charcoal Wood becomes charcoal when it is burnt in a large bonfire. Air is kept out of the fire by carefully piling up the wood. The bonfire has to be kept burning very slowly for a long time. Charcoal is full of a material called carbon. This is used in working iron into steel. A Viking blacksmith used charcoal in his forge.

Drapa A poem composed by a skald (poet) in praise of a chief or king. The poet would expect a rich reward for praising the king's courage in battle and his generosity to his followers.

Flax A plant with blue flowers. Its seeds are crushed to make linseed oil. Fibres from the stems were used by the Vikings to make linen cloth.

Gothi A gothi was a local chief in Iceland. He was the magistrate for his district. This meant that he decided who was right and who was wrong when people came to him with a lawsuit. He was also the temple priest. A gothi was a very important man.

Heathen People who are not Christian are called heathens. The Vikings were heathen long after most people in the rest of Europe had become Christian.

High-seat pillars. A high-seat was the seat in the middle of the benches along the long walls of a Viking house. It was the place of honour. The owner of the house sat in one high-seat, and his chief guest sat opposite him. We do not know exactly what a high-seat looked like, but two wooden pillars, probably richly carved, were set up on either side of the high-seat. These pillars were believed to be sacred.

Jarl A wealthy landowner and chieftain.

Karl A free-born man. Some karls were rich and some were very poor. Craftsmen, soldiers, farmers and traders were all karls.

Lawsuit When people quarrel and go to a law court to have the quarrel settled, they are said to bring a lawsuit to court. The Vikings often took their quarrels to a court. Usually, the person who was proved to be wrong had to give silver to the person who won the lawsuit.

Parley A parley takes place when a battle is stopped for a short time so that the leaders can talk about making peace. When the Vikings held up a white shield it was a signal for the fighting to stop for a parley. If the leaders could not agree, the fighting would start again.

Runes The only kind of writing that the Vikings used was done in runes. The runic alphabet was invented in northern Europe about 2000 years ago, before the Viking Age. The letters were written in straight lines, not curves, so that they could be cut on wooden sticks that were carried by messengers. Runes were also carved on gravestones, and they would often be used to write the name of the owner or maker on a

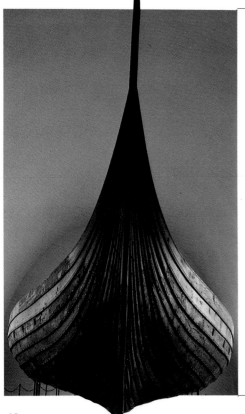

THE GOKSTAD SHIP

The Gokstad ship was discovered in 1880, in a burial mound at the Gokstad farm in Norway. The burial ground is near the sea. The ship was buried in a thick layer of damp blue clay. This preserved the wood, which would have decayed if it had been in dry soil. A man who was about 50 years old had been buried in the ship in about the year 900.

The Gokstad ship was a sturdy sea-going vessel about 23 metres (75 feet) long. It was rowed by 16 pairs of oars. The remains of 64 round wooden shields were found with it. They had been hung on a shield rack along the sides of the ship. The man had been buried in a wooden burial chamber built in the ship. The things he would need to use in his new life had been buried with him.

Parts of a bed were found, with pieces of wool and silk cloth. There were harnesses for horses and a games board. Also in the ship were 6 other beds, a tent, the skeletons of 12 horses and 6 dogs, and the skeleton and feathers of a peacock. A large cooking pot and kitchen utensils were also found. Three small rowing boats were buried alongside the Gokstad ship.

Silver coin from Birka in Sweden.

sword, comb or other object. The Vikings thought that runes were magic and used them to write spells.

Shieling A small hut built in the mountains for people to live in during the summer months, when cattle and sheep were driven up to mountain pastures.

Skald A skald was a Viking poet who traveled from one country to another, living at the courts of famous chiefs and kings. Skalds composed poems in praise of their host, and knew by heart many poems about the heroes of old. Skalds recited poems to entertain the men of the court after the evening meal. They were also fighting men and traders.

Soapstone This is a kind of stone that feels soapy or greasy when you touch it. It is soft and can be easily carved into bowls and ornaments.

Stave A piece of wood cut in a curve and fitted together with other staves to make a cask or barrel. The ends of the staves were fitted into a round wooden top and base. Iron bands were put around the cask to hold the staves together.

Thrall A slave. The Vikings were slave traders. They captured

THE OSEBERG SHIP

The Oseberg ship was found in 1904 when a big burial mound was dug up near the Oseberg farm in Slagan, Norway. It is on the west side of the Oslofjord. This ship was also covered with damp clay, which preserved the wood. It is 21.5 meters (about 70 feet) long, and was built for rowing and sailing near the coast, not for long sea voyages.

It was not as sturdy as the Gokstad ship. Its prow and stern rise up high and end in spirals. On the prow is a serpent's head with eyes. Both prow and stern are decorated with carvings of "Gripping Beasts". There are 15 pairs of oars and both the oars and the mast were made of pine. The ship itself was made of oak. An oak gang-plank and two large wooden casks were found.

A wooden burial chamber had been built on the ship. In it lay the skeletons of an elderly queen and her young girl attendant. The queen was probably Asa, the grandmother of the famous king Harald Fairhair. Everything the queen could need for her new life was buried with her. Beds were provided with pillows, quilts and blankets. All kinds of kitchen and farm equipment were also buried, including wooden spades, a hand-mill for grinding corn, a frying pan and knives and axes.

The bodies of 15 horses, four dogs and an ox were found. Wheat, hazelnuts, walnuts and apples were put in for food. In massive oak chests there were lamp stands and weaving equipment. Three beautifully carved sledges and a carved wagon were also found.

people from other countries to sell as slaves in their market towns. Among the people they captured were Slavs from the south Baltic coasts. The word "Slav" became our word "slave".

Thresh After the wheat and barley had been harvested, the ears of corn were heaped on the floor of a barn and beaten with a wooden tool called a flail. This beating was called threshing. It made the grains of corn fall out of their protective outer coverings, called husks.

Tribute Silver or gold given to Viking armies by other countries. Tribute was paid to stop the armies from attacking and raiding a country.

Wattle and daub In the Viking Age the walls of many houses were made of a frame of wooden

twigs or sticks (wattles), plastered over with handfuls of wet clay mixed with dung or chopped straw. The clay was called "daub". When the clay dried, the wattle and daub made a thick, strong wall.

Winnow After corn was threshed it was tossed into the air so that the wind could blow away the light husks. The heavy grains fell to the ground. This was called 'winnowing'.

Yule Another word for Christmas. It comes from the name of the Viking winter feast, Jolablot, meaning "Yule blood" This feast took place in mid-January and lasted for 12 days. Animals and sometimes men were killed as sacrifices to the gods so that they would give people good crops in the coming season.

Index

ACKNOWLEDGEMENTS

Photographs: Half title, Werner Forman; Contents page, Universitets Old-saksamling, Oslo, Werner Forman, Robert Harding Associates; Page 7 Werner Forman (top), National Travel Association of Denmark; 8 Historiska Museum, Stockholm (top), Spectrum; 9 Werner Forman; 10 Werner Forman (top), Universitets Oldsaksamling, Oslo; 11 Werner Forman; 14 Werner Forman (top), Michael Holford (center); 15 Werner Forman; 16 Werner Forman; 17 Michael Holford, Historiska Museum, Stockholm (center); 18 Robert Harding Associates (top), Werner Forman; 19 Picturepoint, Universitets Oldsaksamling, Oslo (top right); 20 Michael Holford (bottom); 21 Werner Forman, Universitets Oldsaksamling, Oslo (bottom); 24 Universitets Oldsaksamling, Oslo; 25 Werner Forman (top), British Museum; 26 Werner Forman; 27 Werner Forman; 29 Werner Forman; 30 Michael Holford; 31 Picturepoint (top); 34 Werner Forman; 35 Werner Forman; 38 Manuscript Institute of Iceland; 39 Picturepoint; 40 Werner Forman; 41 Michael Holford (top), Universitets Oldsaksamling, Oslo; 42 Werner Forman; 43 Werner Forman.

Picture Research: Anne Houghton.

AD 800

VIKINGS

789 First Viking attacks on England

834 Vikings raid the great market town of Dorestad in the Netherlands

850 Swedes begin to settle in East Baltic and Russia

860 Discovery of Iceland

874 First settlers in Iceland

886 King Alfred defeats Guthrum; Danes allowed to settle in the Danelaw

900

911 Scandinavians settle in Normandy

982 Eirik the Red discovers Greenland

1000

995–1000 Olaf Tryggvason, King of Norway

1003 Leif Eiriksson lands in North America

1030 King Olaf of Norway killed at Battle of Stiklastad

1047 Harald Hardrada becomes King of Norway

1066 Harald Hardrada killed at Battle of Stamford Bridge in England, by King Harold of England. Duke William of Normandy kills Harold of England at the Battle of Hastings and becomes King William I of England

1066

EUROPE

800 Charlemagne, King of the Franks, is crowned Holy Roman Emperor in western Europe

843 Treaty of Verdun divides the Frankish empire between Charlemagne's grandsons

871 Alfred the Great becomes King of Wessex

906 Magyars from the East invade Germany

911 Charles the Simple gives the Viking leader Rollo land in Normandy

955 Otto I of Germany ends the westward advance of the Magyars at the Battle of Lech

987 Hugh Capet elected King of France; foundation of the Capetian Dynasty

1002 Ethelred II of England orders the slaughter of all Danish settlers in southern England

1042 Edward the Confessor becomes King of England

1066 Edward the Confessor dies, Harold II crowned King of England

ISLAM

803 Harun al-Raschid, Caliph of
   Baghdad destroys the Barmakids,
   the Persian Dynasty that
   administers his empire

827 Arabs begin conquest of the
   islands of Sicily and Sardinia
838 Arabs attack Marseilles and
   establish a base in southern Italy
843 Arabs capture Messina

859 Arabs complete conquest of
   Sicily
869 Arabs capture Malta

888 Arabs establish a camp in
   Provence in France

922 Fatimid Dynasty seizes
   Morocco

970 The Seljuk Turks become
   Muslim and occupy most of Persia
980 Arabs begin settling along the
   eastern coast of Africa
983 The Caliph of Egypt rules over
   Palestine and southern Syria

1054 Abdallah ben Yassim begins
   the Muslim conquest of West
   Africa
1055 The Seljuks seize Baghdad
1061 Muslim Almoravid Dynasty in
   North Africa; later conquers
   Spain

ELSEWHERE

821 Conquest of Tibet by the Chinese

832 Nanchao, a state in south China
   destroys the kingdom of the
   Pyu people, the earliest known
   inhabitants of Burma

850 Acropolis of Zimbabwe built in
   eastern Africa

900 Mayas emigrate to the Yucatan
   Peninsula of Mexico
907–960 End of T'ang Dynasty in
   China; civil war follows

920–1050 Golden Age of Ghana
   empire
939 Civil wars break out in Japan
960 Sung Dynasty in China

987 New Mayan empire established
   in Yucatan with its capital at
   Mayapan
995–1028 Golden age of the arts in
   Japan
1000s Gunpowder perfected by the
   Chinese

1043 Mandingo empire of Jenne
   founded in West Africa

**AD
800**

900

1000

1066